HOW TO DRAW MECHA ROBOTS AND BATTLE FANTASY FIGURES

Mark Bergin

BOOK HOUSE

SALARIYA

Published in Great Britain in 2007 by
Book House, an imprint of
The Salariya Book Company Ltd
25 Marlborough Place, Brighton BN1 1UB

1 3 5 7 9 8 6 4 2

Please visit our website at **www.book-house.co.uk**
for **free** electronic versions of:
You Wouldn't Want to Be an Egyptian Mummy!
You Wouldn't Want to Be a Roman Gladiator!
Avoid Joining Shackleton's Polar Expedition!
Avoid Sailing on a 19th-Century Whaling Ship!

Author: Mark Bergin was born in Hastings, England, in 1961.
He studied at Eastbourne College of Art, and specialises in
historical reconstructions, aviation and maritime subjects.
He lives in Bexhill-on-Sea with his wife and children.

Editors: Rob Walker, Stephen Haynes

PB ISBN: 978-1-905638-50-5

A CIP catalogue record for this
book is available from the
British Library.

Printed and bound in China.
Printed on paper from
sustainable sources.

WORCESTERSHIRE COUNTY COUNCIL	
410	
Bertrams	30.07.07
J743.8	£10.99
PE	

**WARNING: Fixatives should be
used only under adult supervision.**

Contents

Making a start

Learning to draw is about looking and seeing. Keep practising, and get to know your subject. Use a sketchbook to make quick sketches. Start by doodling, and experiment with shapes and patterns. There are many ways to draw; this book shows one method. Visit art galleries, look at artists' drawings, see how friends draw, but above all, find your own way.

Combat mecha

Remember that practice makes perfect. If it looks wrong, start again. Keep working at it — the more you draw, the more you will learn.

Security droid

Giant mecha

Flying mecha

Fantasy mecha

Perspective

If you look at any object from different viewpoints, you will see that the part that is closest to you will look larger, and the part furthest away from you will look smaller. Drawing in perspective is a way of creating a feeling of space — of showing three dimensions on a flat surface.

A view from above can be achieved using a single vanishing point.

The vanishing point (V.P.) is the place in a perspective drawing where parallel lines appear to meet. The position of the vanishing point depends on the viewer's eye level. Sometimes a low viewpoint can give your drawing added drama.

✳ V.P.

V.P. ✳

Two-point perspective drawing

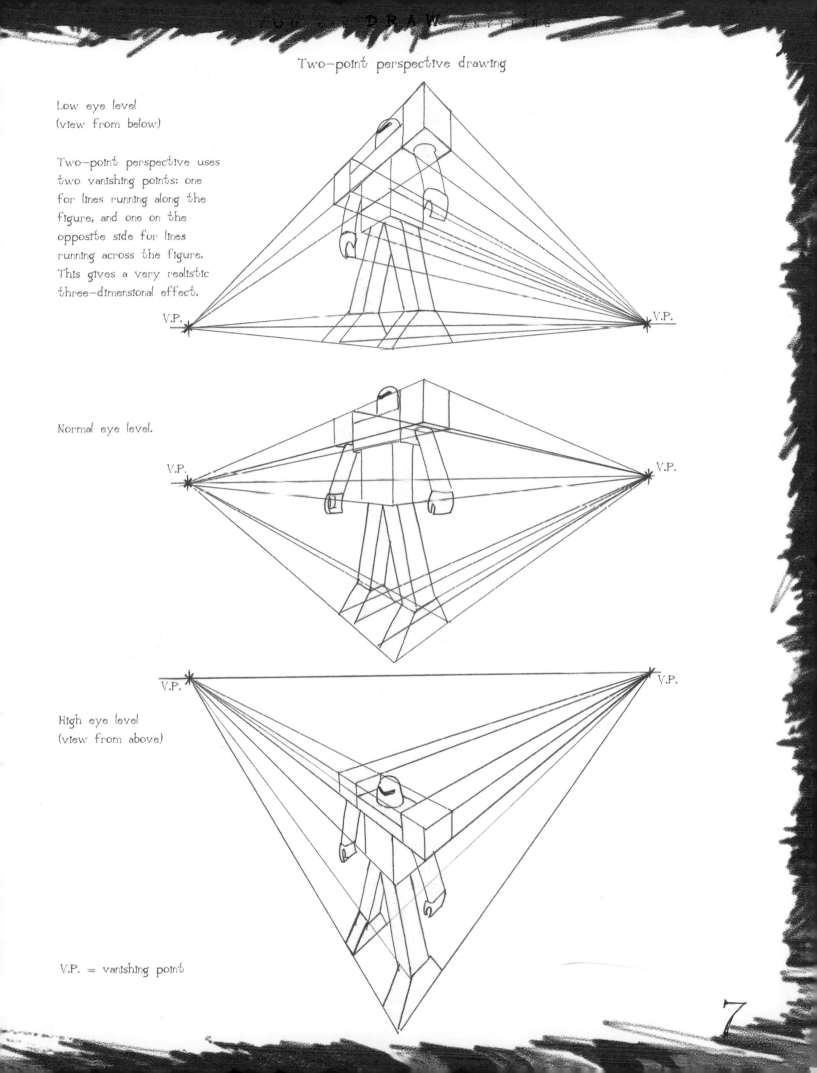

Low eye level
(view from below)

Two-point perspective uses
two vanishing points: one
for lines running along the
figure, and one on the
opposite side for lines
running across the figure.
This gives a very realistic
three-dimensional effect.

V.P.   V.P.

Normal eye level.

V.P.   V.P.

V.P.   V.P.

High eye level
(view from above)

V.P. = vanishing point

7

Drawing tools

Here are just a few of the many tools that you can use for drawing. Let your imagination go, and have fun experimenting with all the different marks you can make.

Each grade of **pencil** makes a different mark, from fine, grey lines through to soft, black ones. Hard pencils are graded as H, 2H, 3H, 4H, 5H and 6H (the hardest). An HB pencil is ideal for general sketching. Soft pencils are graded from B, 2B, 3B, 4B, 5B to 6B (the softest and blackest).

Watercolour pencils come in many different colours and make a line similar to an HB pencil. But paint over your finished drawing with clean water, and the lines will soften and run.

It is less messy and easier to achieve a fine line with a **charcoal pencil** than a charcoal stick. Create soft tones by smudging lines with your finger. **Ask an adult** to spray the drawing with fixative to prevent further smudging.

Pastels are brittle sticks of powdered colour. They blend and smudge easily and are ideal for quick sketches. Pastel drawings work well on textured, coloured paper. **Ask an adult** to spray your finished drawing with fixative.

Experiment with **finger painting**. Your fingerprints make exciting patterns and textures. Use your fingers to smudge soft pencil, charcoal and pastel lines.

Ballpoint pens are very useful for sketching and making notes. Make different tones by building up layers of shading.

A **mapping pen** has to be dipped into bottled ink to fill the nib. Different nib shapes make different marks. Try putting a diluted ink wash over parts of the finished drawing.

Draughtsmen's pens and specialist **art pens** can produce extremely fine lines and are ideal for creating surface texture. A variety of pen nibs are available which produce different widths of line.

Felt—tip pens are ideal for quick sketches. If the ink is not waterproof, try drawing on wet paper and see what happens.

Broad—nibbed **marker pens** make interesting lines and are good for large, bold sketches. Try using a black pen for the main sketch and a grey one to block in areas of shadow.

Paintbrushes are shaped differently to make different marks. Japanese brushes are soft and produce beautiful flowing lines. Large sable brushes are good for painting a wash over a line drawing. Fine brushes are good for drawing delicate lines.

Materials

Try using different types of drawing papers and materials. Experiment with charcoal, wax crayons and pastels. All pens, from felt—tips to ballpoints, will make interesting marks. Try drawing with pen and ink on wet paper.

Ink silhouette

Felt—tips come in a range of line widths. The wider pens are good for filling in large areas of flat tone.

Remember, the best equipment and materials will not necessarily make the best drawing — practice will!

Pencil drawings can include a vast amount of detail and tone. Try experimenting with the different grades of pencil to get different types of tonal effects in your drawing.

Lines drawn in **ink** cannot be erased, so keep your ink drawings sketchy and less rigid. Don't worry about mistakes, as these can be lost in the drawing as it develops.

Hatching

Cross-hatching

Adding different tonal areas to a drawing with an ink pen can be difficult. Use solid ink for the darkest areas and cross-hatching (straight lines criss-crossing each other) for dark tones. Use hatching (straight lines running parallel to each other) for midtones, and keep the lightest areas empty.

*When the use of light and shade in a drawing is very dramatic, artists call it **chiaroscuro** — an Italian word that means 'light-dark'.

11

Drawing a scene

To make your mecha robot drawing even more exciting, you can place the mecha in a scene. This can give your drawing added drama and a sense of action. This example shows the mecha robots in a cityscape, but you can use your imagination to draw them in any situation you like.

First draw a box with a horizon line running through it, then draw the construction lines of the mecha robots themselves. Any vanishing points (see page 6) should be on the horizon line.

Use the horizon line and perspective to draw the square shapes of the city buildings. Add detail to the mecha robots. Sketch in simple shapes for objects such as cars and people.

Once you have the basic shape of the drawing, you can start to add windows to the buildings and put in the final details on the bodies of the mecha robots.

13

Security droid

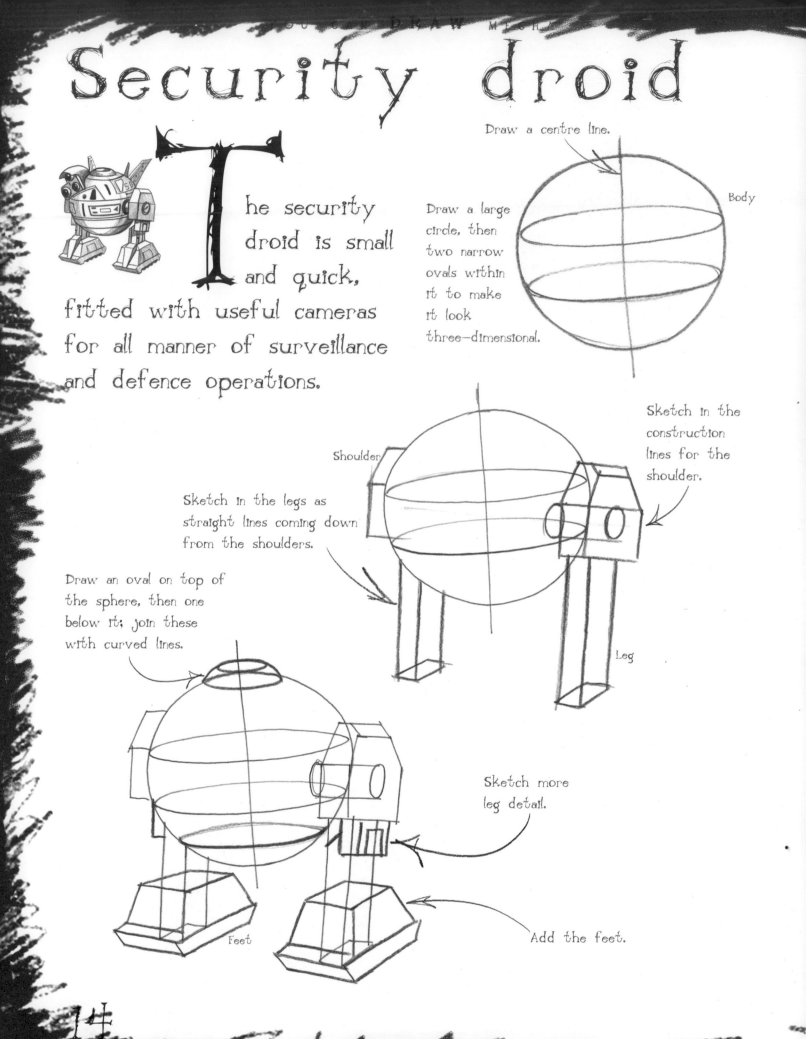

The security droid is small and quick, fitted with useful cameras for all manner of surveillance and defence operations.

Draw a centre line.

Draw a large circle, then two narrow ovals within it to make it look three-dimensional.

Body

Shoulder

Sketch in the construction lines for the shoulder.

Sketch in the legs as straight lines coming down from the shoulders.

Draw an oval on top of the sphere, then one below it; join these with curved lines.

Leg

Sketch more leg detail.

Feet

Add the feet.

Camera unit

A curved line coming from the top of the robot marks the top of the camera unit.

The fins on the rear of the bot are drawn with straight lines, forming an almost triangular shape.

Draw ovals for the lenses of the camera unit.

Draw rectangles and lines on the body. Remember to curve the lines to keep it looking spherical.

Wheels

Add the wheels on the feet with semicircles.

This detail looks a little like circuit boards. Add some to your drawing to make it look more robotic.

Shade in the lenses of the cameras, adding a highlight to each one for the reflection in the glass.

Shade in the areas where light will not reach.

Complete the detail of the feet.

Complete the shoulders of the security bot.

The straight edges make shading the darkest areas easier.

15

Giant mecha

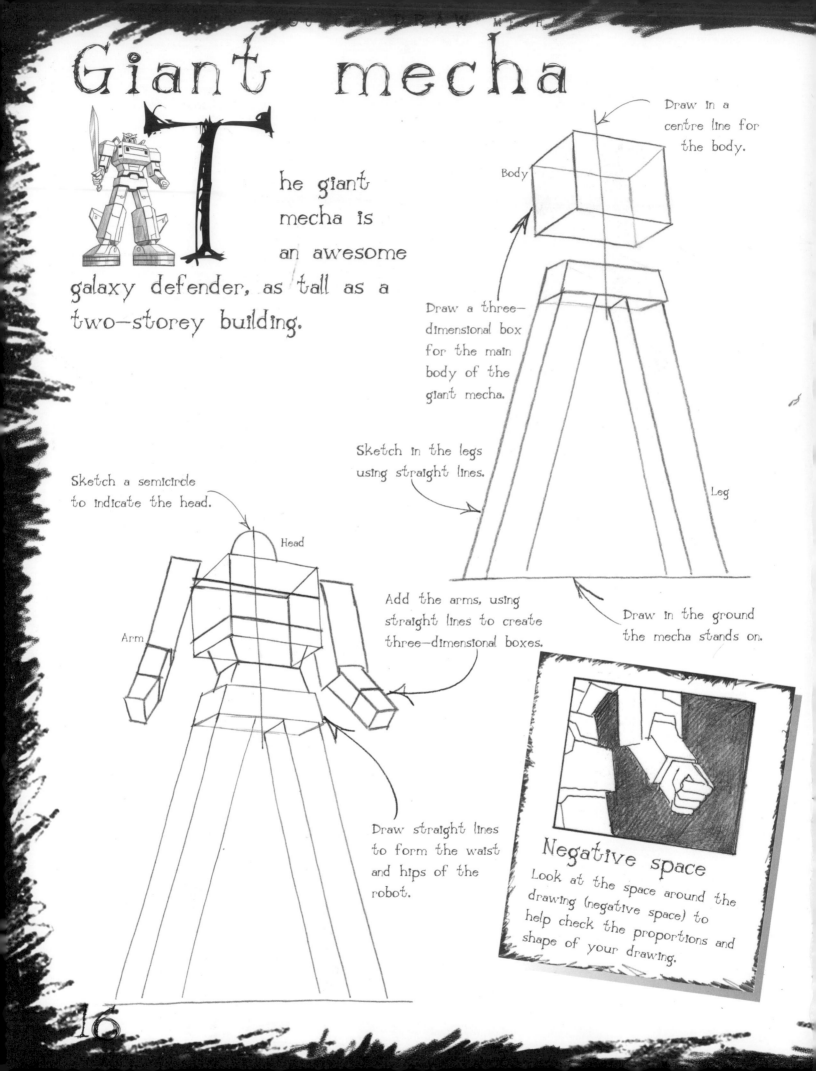

The giant mecha is an awesome galaxy defender, as tall as a two-storey building.

Draw in a centre line for the body.

Body

Draw a three-dimensional box for the main body of the giant mecha.

Sketch in the legs using straight lines.

Leg

Sketch a semicircle to indicate the head.

Head

Arm

Add the arms, using straight lines to create three-dimensional boxes.

Draw in the ground the mecha stands on.

Draw straight lines to form the waist and hips of the robot.

Negative space

Look at the space around the drawing (negative space) to help check the proportions and shape of your drawing.

Sketch in the sword.

Sketch the details of the face.

*Remove your construction lines once you are sure you have finished with them.

Add straight lines to the tops of the arms to form the shoulders.

Using your construction lines as a guide, draw in the hands of the mecha.

Finish the detail of the head.

Shade in one side of the sword.

Draw two large rectangles for the base of the feet, then add the ankle joints and main areas of leg.

Add the detail to the mecha; straight lines on its surface show how it is made mechanically.

Decide on where the light is coming from, then shade the areas where it would not reach.

17

Flying mecha

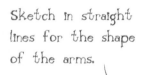

The flying mecha is an aerial combat drone. Its wings and rocket boosters allow it to travel at terrific speeds and combat any airborne threat.

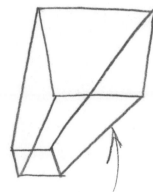

Begin the flying mecha by drawing a simple box in perspective.

Head

Draw an oval for the head.

Draw a centre line through the perspective box.

Body

Sketch in straight lines for the shape of the arms.

Add construction lines for the hands.

Arm

Legs

Outline the shape of the legs by drawing straight lines to form boxes.

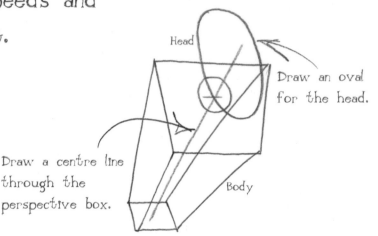

Composition
Framing your drawing with squares or rectangles can make it look completely different.

Feet   Add the feet.

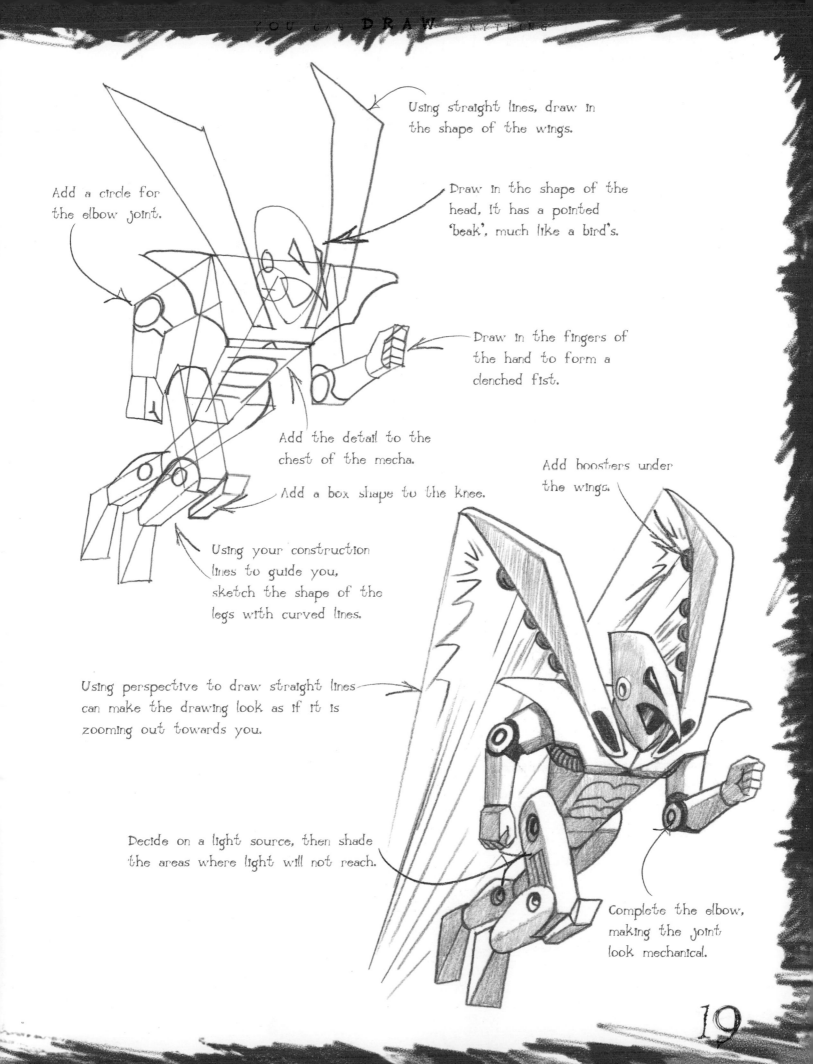

Using straight lines, draw in the shape of the wings.

Draw in the shape of the head, It has a pointed 'beak', much like a bird's.

Add a circle for the elbow joint.

Draw in the fingers of the hand to form a clenched fist.

Add the detail to the chest of the mecha.

Add a box shape to the knee.

Add boosters under the wings.

Using your construction lines to guide you, sketch the shape of the legs with curved lines.

Using perspective to draw straight lines can make the drawing look as if it is zooming out towards you.

Decide on a light source, then shade the areas where light will not reach.

Complete the elbow, making the joint look mechanical.

19

Explorer robot

Draw a large oval.

Explorer mecha are droids sent to hazardous worlds all over the galaxy. This one has heavy tank tracks for any terrain, and extendable tools for taking samples from the surface.

Draw a simple perspective box for the base of the exploration robot.

Perspective box

Draw two curved lines going diagonally across the large oval.

The joint between the top of the mecha and the bottom is made up of curved and straight lines.

Draw a line about halfway up the box, then draw diagonal lines to the top and bottom of the perspective box to form the front end of the explorer mecha.

Draw an oval on the top of the box. Add curved lines from its edges up to a smaller oval.

Add ovals for the wheels, drawing a smaller curved line inside them to make them look three-dimensional.

Track

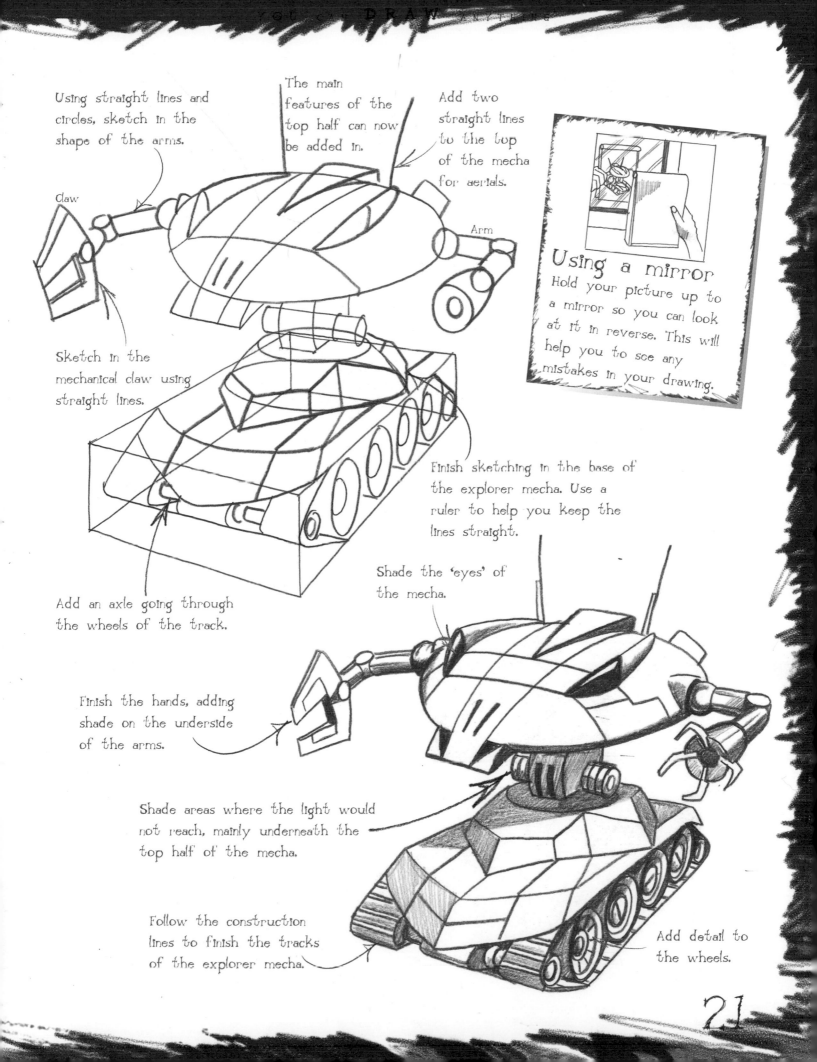

Using straight lines and circles, sketch in the shape of the arms.

Claw

The main features of the top half can now be added in.

Add two straight lines to the top of the mecha for aerials.

Arm

Using a mirror
Hold your picture up to a mirror so you can look at it in reverse. This will help you to see any mistakes in your drawing.

Sketch in the mechanical claw using straight lines.

Finish sketching in the base of the explorer mecha. Use a ruler to help you keep the lines straight.

Add an axle going through the wheels of the track.

Shade the 'eyes' of the mecha.

Finish the hands, adding shade on the underside of the arms.

Shade areas where the light would not reach, mainly underneath the top half of the mecha.

Follow the construction lines to finish the tracks of the explorer mecha.

Add detail to the wheels.

21

Combat mecha

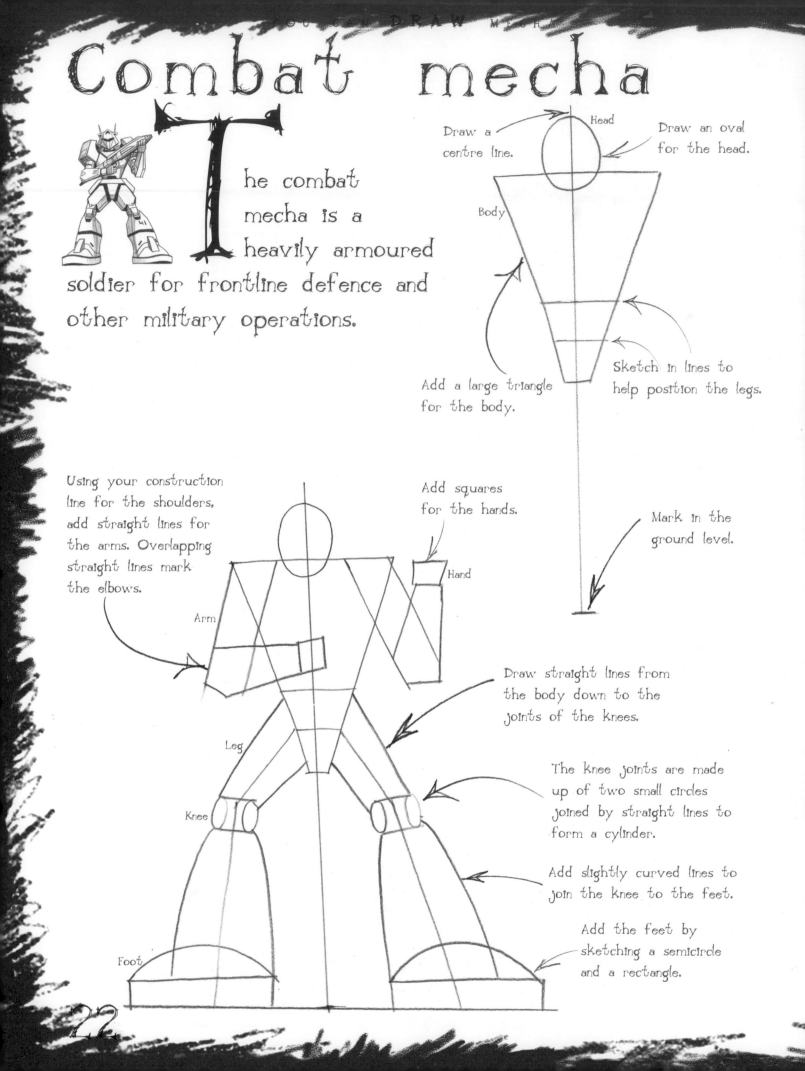

The combat mecha is a heavily armoured soldier for frontline defence and other military operations.

Draw a centre line.

Head

Draw an oval for the head.

Body

Add a large triangle for the body.

Sketch in lines to help position the legs.

Using your construction line for the shoulders, add straight lines for the arms. Overlapping straight lines mark the elbows.

Add squares for the hands.

Hand

Arm

Mark in the ground level.

Draw straight lines from the body down to the joints of the knees.

Leg

The knee joints are made up of two small circles joined by straight lines to form a cylinder.

Knee

Add slightly curved lines to join the knee to the feet.

Add the feet by sketching a semicircle and a rectangle.

Foot

Helmet

Draw in the helmet.

Gun

Hand

Draw a straight construction line to place the gun, then add the straight lines and circles.

Complete the shape of the arms, adding geometric shapes for the armour.

Add the armour around the waist. It is all drawn with straight lines, so a ruler will help.

Add the detail to the body, making it look as futuristic as possible.

Follow the construction lines to finish drawing the gun.

Feet

Add curved lines to the bottom of the feet.

Continue following the construction lines to complete the legs, adding in detail as you go.

Shade the inside of the legs.

23

Human mecha

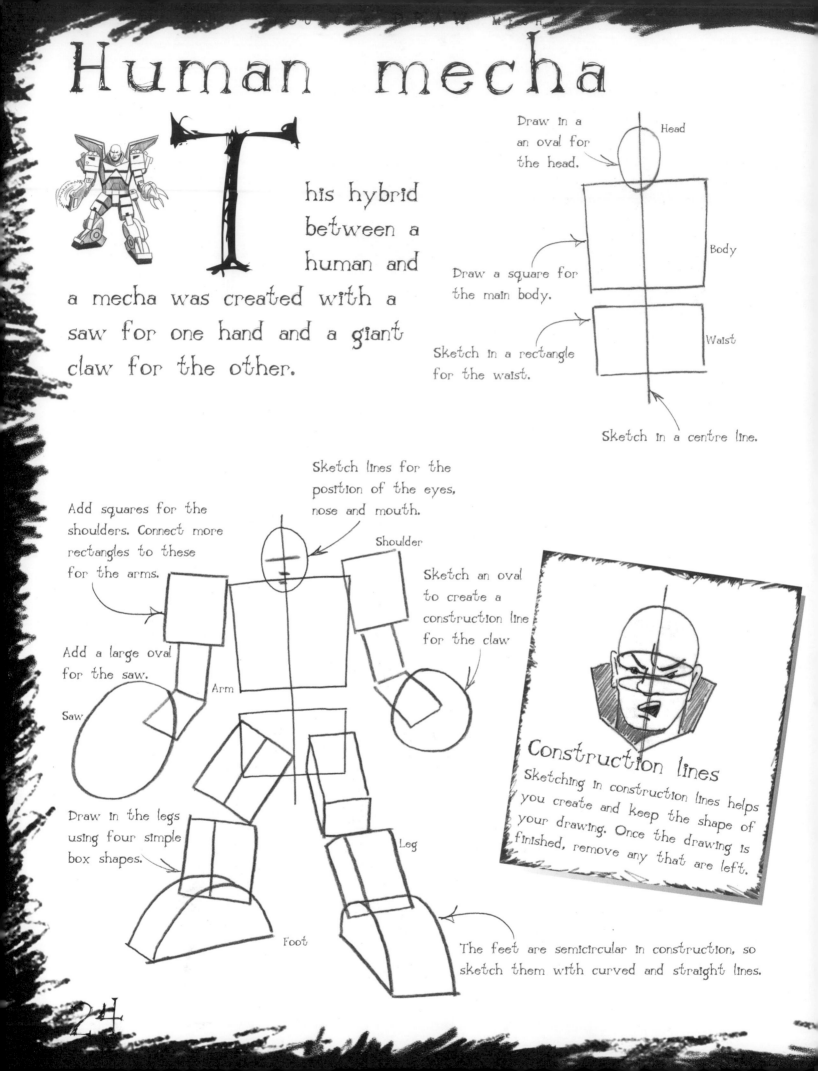

This hybrid between a human and a mecha was created with a saw for one hand and a giant claw for the other.

Draw in a an oval for the head.

Head

Draw a square for the main body.

Body

Sketch in a rectangle for the waist.

Waist

Sketch in a centre line.

Sketch lines for the position of the eyes, nose and mouth.

Add squares for the shoulders. Connect more rectangles to these for the arms.

Shoulder

Sketch an oval to create a construction line for the claw

Add a large oval for the saw.

Saw

Arm

Draw in the legs using four simple box shapes.

Leg

Construction lines

Sketching in construction lines helps you create and keep the shape of your drawing. Once the drawing is finished, remove any that are left.

Foot

The feet are semicircular in construction, so sketch them with curved and straight lines.

Add wings on the back of the mecha.

Sketch in the detail of the main body. Use straight lines to create a 'chest' and 'stomach'.

Using the construction lines to help, start drawing the mechanical claw.

Add the joint of the leg.

Complete the detail of the face.

Add details to the feet using circles and squares.

Add more detail to the arms to make them look more mechanical.

Add the jagged edge of the saw.

Use the construction lines as a guide to complete the legs.

Finish the claw.

Shade areas where the light will not reach, to give the drawing a three-dimensional effect.

Land walker

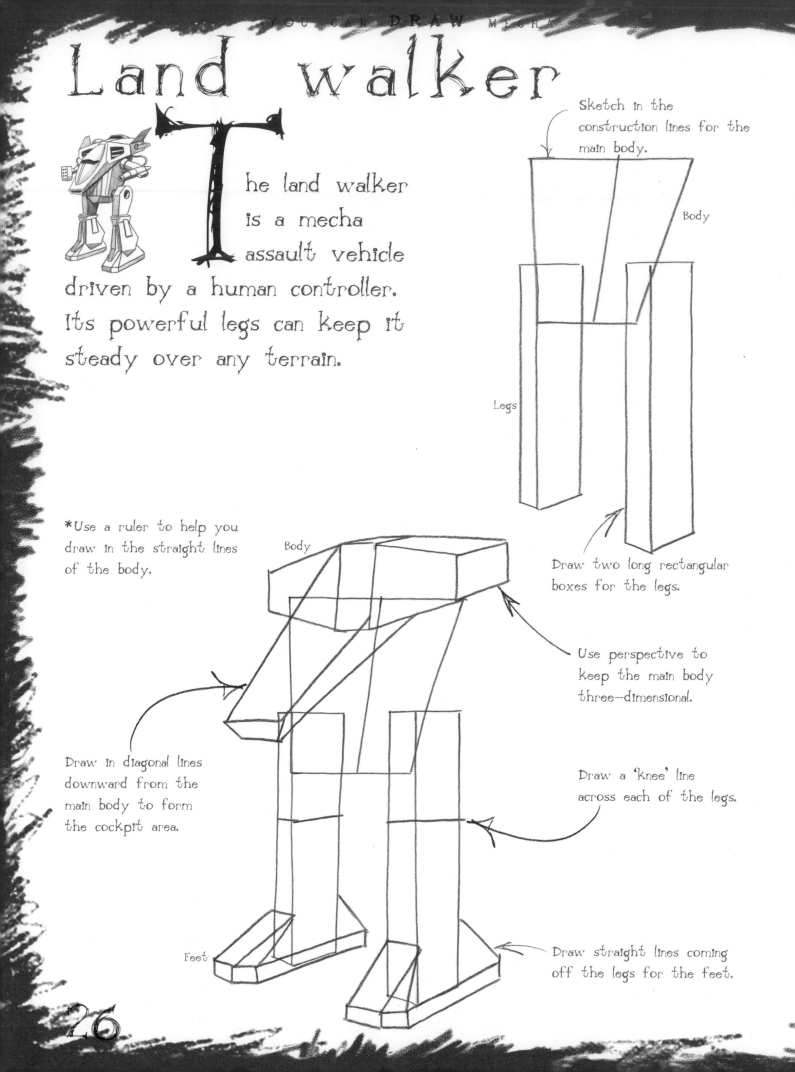

The land walker is a mecha assault vehicle driven by a human controller. Its powerful legs can keep it steady over any terrain.

Sketch in the construction lines for the main body.

Body

Legs

Draw two long rectangular boxes for the legs.

*Use a ruler to help you draw in the straight lines of the body.

Body

Use perspective to keep the main body three-dimensional.

Draw in diagonal lines downward from the main body to form the cockpit area.

Draw a 'knee' line across each of the legs.

Feet

Draw straight lines coming off the legs for the feet.

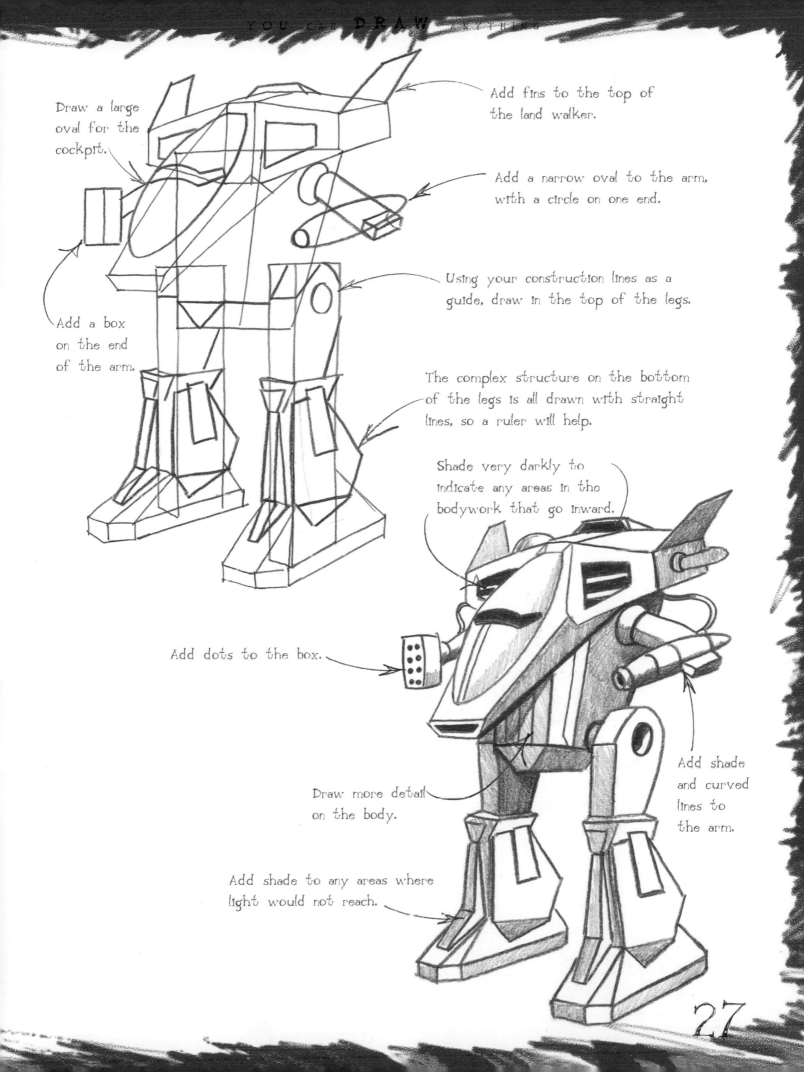

Draw a large oval for the cockpit.

Add fins to the top of the land walker.

Add a narrow oval to the arm, with a circle on one end.

Add a box on the end of the arm.

Using your construction lines as a guide, draw in the top of the legs.

The complex structure on the bottom of the legs is all drawn with straight lines, so a ruler will help.

Shade very darkly to indicate any areas in the bodywork that go inward.

Add dots to the box.

Draw more detail on the body.

Add shade and curved lines to the arm.

Add shade to any areas where light would not reach.

Mutant mecha

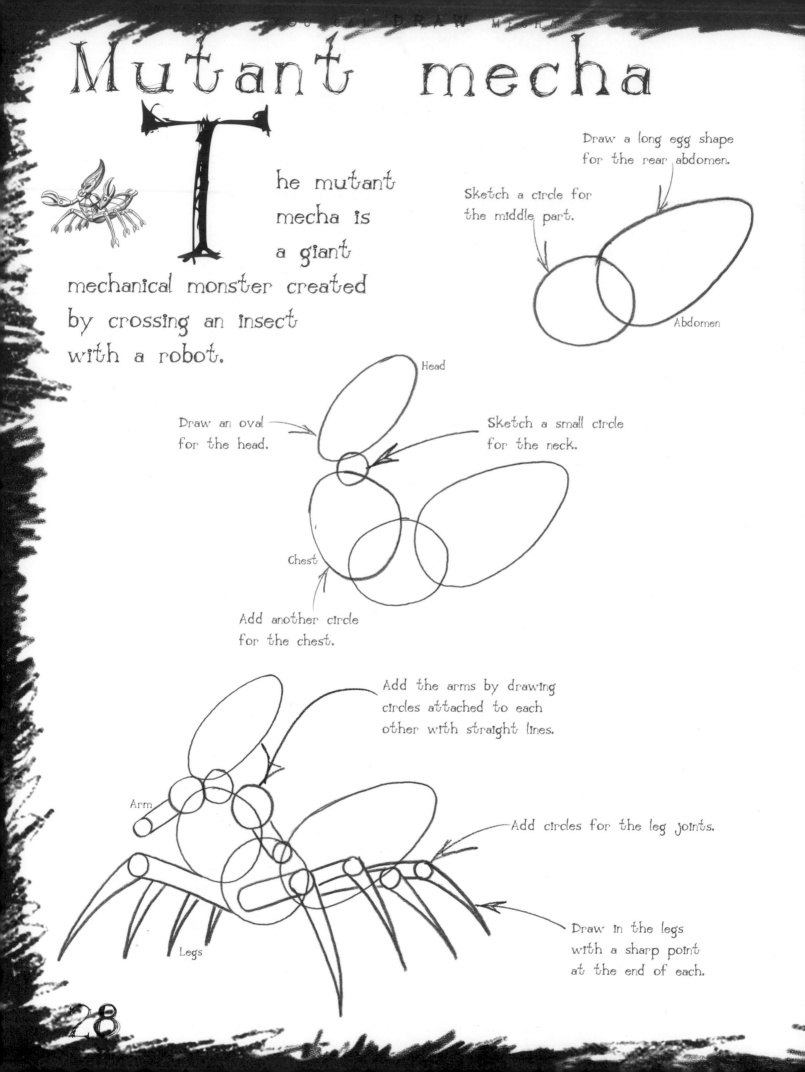

The mutant mecha is a giant mechanical monster created by crossing an insect with a robot.

Draw a long egg shape for the rear abdomen.

Sketch a circle for the middle part.

Abdomen

Head

Draw an oval for the head.

Sketch a small circle for the neck.

Chest

Add another circle for the chest.

Add the arms by drawing circles attached to each other with straight lines.

Arm

Add circles for the leg joints.

Draw in the legs with a sharp point at the end of each.

Legs

Add the eyes.

Draw the shape of the head using curved lines.

Draw in a claw using curved lines.

Add a sharp claw to the rear of the abdomen.

Add the feet.

Draw a curved line down from the neck to the body. Use this to help you draw in the chest.

Add detail to the head.

Draw curved lines on the abdomen to make it look three-dimensional.

Add more detail to the face, shading the eyes.

Shade in the areas where light would not reach.

Finish the detail on the main body.

Add a shaded line to each leg to give a shiny, metallic look.

Fantasy mecha

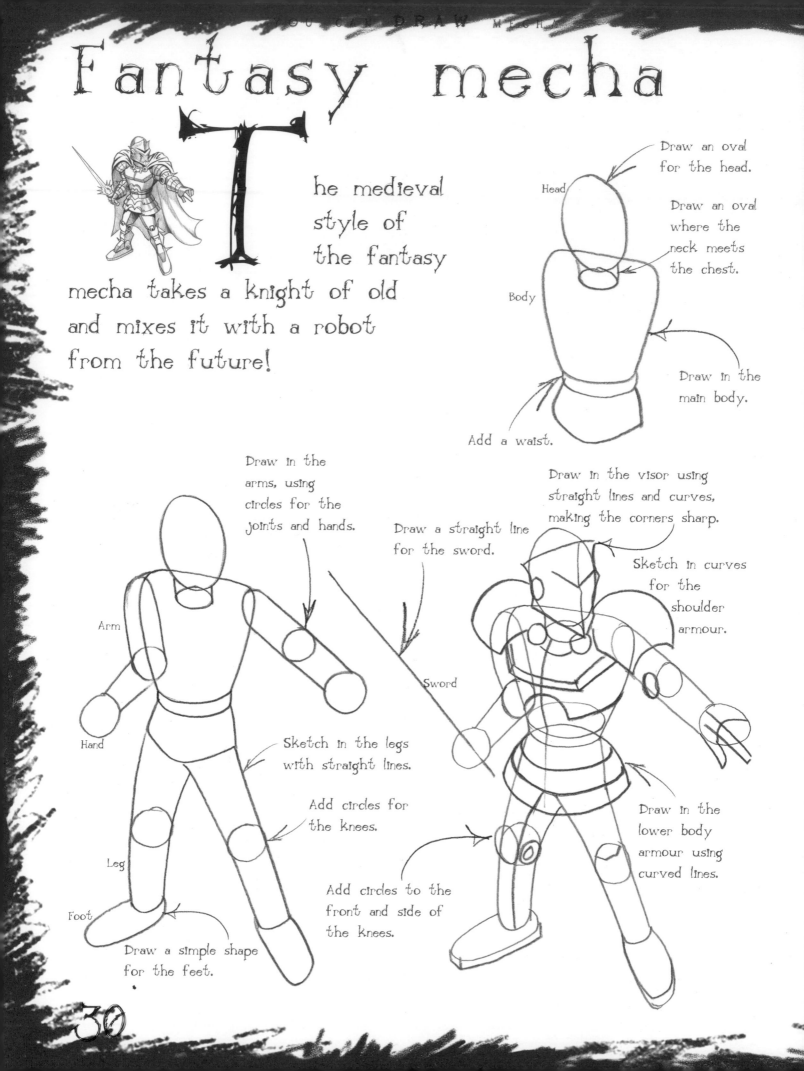

The medieval style of the fantasy mecha takes a knight of old and mixes it with a robot from the future!

Draw an oval for the head.

Head

Draw an oval where the neck meets the chest.

Body

Draw in the main body.

Add a waist.

Draw in the arms, using circles for the joints and hands.

Draw a straight line for the sword.

Draw in the visor using straight lines and curves, making the corners sharp.

Sketch in curves for the shoulder armour.

Arm

Hand

Sword

Sketch in the legs with straight lines.

Add circles for the knees.

Leg

Foot

Add circles to the front and side of the knees.

Draw a simple shape for the feet.

Draw in the lower body armour using curved lines.

Complete the sword with straight lines for the blade and curves for the hilt.

Add the eye slit to the visor.

Add a spike coming from the elbow.

Draw in the armour cuffs with straight lines and curves to make a conical shape.

Draw in the hands using the circular construction lines as guides

Sketch in the cape using long, curved lines.

Cape

Shade areas of the helmet and visor, to give them a metallic look.

Ankle

Add detail to the ankle areas.

Finish the laser sword.

Finish any detail on the armour and remove any unwanted construction lines.

Add detail to the surface of the armour. Small circles can look like bolts holding it together.

Shade where light will not reach.

31

Glossary

Chiaroscuro The use of light and dark in a drawing.

Composition The positioning of a picture on the drawing paper.

Construction lines Structural lines used in the early stages of a drawing, and usually erased later.

Cross-hatching A series of criss-crossing lines used to add shade to a drawing.

Fixative A type of resin used to spray over a finished drawing to prevent smudging. **It should only be used by an adult.**

Hatching A series of parallel lines used to add shade to a drawing.

Light source The direction from which the light seems to come in a drawing.

Negative space The space around and between the parts of a drawing.

Proportion The correct relationship of scale between parts of a drawing.

Reference Photographs or other images used to help produce a drawing, if drawing from life is not possible.

Three-dimensional Having an effect of depth, so as to look lifelike or real.

Vanishing point The place in a perspective drawing where parallel lines appear to meet.

Index